101
Successful PR
Campaign
Tips

LifeTips Book Series

By Mary White
Press Release Guru
LifeTips

LifeTips Book Series
Boston, Massachusetts

LIFETIPS PRESIDENT: Byron White

BOOK SERIES EDITOR: Amanda Smyth

LifeTips.com, Inc.

101 Book Series

77 North Washington Street

Suite 3B

Boston, MA 02114

(617) 227-8800

http://www.LifeTips.com

International Standard Book No. 978-1-60275-038-8

Table of Contents

What will make your story stand out from the hundreds of press releases that appear on any given desk? Well, you've chosen to read this fantastic tip book for one. You've already got that under your belt. Next, you need to apply these tips to your writing. Dedicate yourself to learning the fine art of press release writing from Mary White, the LifeTips Guru on Public Relations and Marketing. Take your style and talent to the next level!

There are millions of press releases floating around. Only a few at any given time might be considered "good," and even fewer are "eye-catching, head-turning, Hey-Joe-Come-Take-A-Look-At-This" great. This book will help prepare you to produce the latter.

To write a really great press release, you need to see the beauty and the substance in your subject matter. You need to believe in what you are writing. Otherwise, the artificiality in your tone will come across to your audience. You can't trick the masses. It's like the difference between regular and diet soda. People can always tell real from fake.

Believe what you are writing and use your superpowers, as the wonderfully brilliant writer that you are, to make your audience believe you. Get your press release noticed! Make your press release more powerful! Everything can be made newsworthy, even those inevitable waterskiing squirrel stories. You just need to believe in the power of your own story. That is half the battle.

Now we move on to the next three-quarters of the battle. There is an art to writing press releases. No news there. There is an art to doing anything if you hope to do it well. Whether a press release is meant to convey critical information pertaining to a nation-altering tragedy, or to announce a television network's winning season line-up, every single press release is important and should be held in the highest regard when being written and distributed.

That tidbit of knowledge takes us up to seven and three-eighths of the battle. We here at LifeTips Editorial care deeply about words. Numbers take something of a back seat.

It is your job to disseminate this great information in a clear, concise and powerfully-written package. You are the messenger, and if you mess up, well, you know what happens to messengers.

I encourage you to dive head first into this tip book. Get all you can from every tip, apply it to your style and become the best public relations guru that you can be. From there you can focus on taking over the world.

Enjoy!

Amanda Smyth
LifeTips Editor

Public relations is both an art and a science, and the field has changed greatly in recent years. Press Releases were originally used to communicate information to reporters, who would then determine whether or not it was newsworthy enough to pass along to consumers.

While media coverage is still a very real part of modern PR, press releases now fill many different functions within an organization's overall public relations plan. PR practitioners are having to re-think the purpose and functions of press releases in the "Web 2.0" world. Press releases have evolved into a direct-to-consumer communications tool. Corporate websites, blogs, online press release distribution, and search engine marketing have made it possible for companies to keep their names in front of consumers with a continuous flow of information at very little cost.

This book is designed to provide practical tips for utilizing press releases as powerful tools for generating publicity in both traditional media outlets and in the online arena. The information contained in this book will benefit small business owners and managers, communications professionals, volunteers for non-profit organizations, and everyone else who wants to learn more about how to generate publicity.

About the Author

Mary Gormandy White has been practicing and teaching public relations and related topics for nearly two decades. A born communicator, she holds graduate and undergraduate degrees in Communication and has experience in both corporate communications and agency PR. She has worked with clients in many fields, including health care, hospitality, publishing, retail, travel, and many others.

In her current role as co-founder of Mobile Technical Institute (www.mobiletechwebsite.com), and MTI Business Solutions, she is able to combine her love for teaching with PR practice. She handles the firm's PR, helps clients with their marketing and PR needs, and teaches a variety of public relations, communication, and general business courses.

1| Advertising and Public Relations Differ in Many Ways

Advertising and public relations may both be used as part of a company's overall marketing strategy, but they are not the same thing. There are a number of differences between advertising and public relations, with the primary differences being (1) control, (2) cost, and (3) credibility.

Advertising is a controlled form of communication, and public relations is uncontrolled. When you purchase advertising space and time, you control the content of the message, where it will appear, and when it appears. With public relations, you do not have the final say regarding when, if, or in what form your message will show up in the media.

Advertising time is purchased, so it can be costly. With advertising, you pay to develop, produce, and place your message. With public relations, you may pay someone to help get the word out about your company to the news media and to prospective customers, but you don't pay for actual placement.

Because no money changes hands to place public relations messages in the media, such messages are often said to have greater credibility than advertising messages. The third party endorsement associated with having a journalist say something great about your company in an article is often viewed more positively than an advertisement that the public knows you paid to create and place.

2| All PR is Marketing, But All Marketing is Not PR

There is a strong association between marketing and public relations. PR is an important part of the marketing mix. The marketing mix is defined as the unique combination of product, price, placement, and promotion that result in the ultimate success of a product or service. Along with advertising, public relations is an important component of the promotion aspect of the marketing mix.

Public relations is a very important technique for spreading the word about your company's products and services. Generating publicity, primarily via writing and submitting news releases to a variety of media outlets, is what people most commonly associate with public relations. However, public relations involves much more that just generating media coverage.

When a company holds an open house to attract past, present, and prospective customers to tour its place of business, the company is hosting a public relations event. When the organization's managing director makes a speech at the local Kiwanis organization's meeting, he or she is engaging in a public relations activity. Every promotional activity that a company engages in that is not a paid advertising placement can be considered to be a part of the public relations component of the marketing mix. Public relations activities are designed to increase awareness of a company's products or services, position it as a socially responsible entity, and to generate goodwill among all groups who affect or are affected by the organization.

3| Connections and Technology are Keys to High Tech PR Success

High tech public relations focuses on technology products and services. This specialization within the field includes public relations activities for many different types of businesses and products, including: computer software, tools for software development, computer hardware, computer security, electronics, online retailing, and many others.

More so than any other field, those involved in high tech public relations have to stay on the forefront of communications technology. To be perceived as a credible resource for high tech product information, publicists specializing in this type of PR must be among the first to adopt and utilize the latest tools for reaching their target publics.

Public relations firms and individuals who specialize in high tech PR cultivate contacts with editors, reporters, bloggers, podcasters, and others who have the ability to influence public awareness and public opinion in the ever-changing high tech marketplace. They are constantly searching for new ways of reaching technology consumers and decision makers, while simultaneously continuing to promote their clients via traditional media outlets and channels. The assistance of a well-connected firm or publicist can be invaluable to high tech manufacturers and developers.

4| Corporate Public Relations Encompasses All Aspects of Corporate Communication

The phrase corporate public relations refers to the unique combination of all PR activities performed for a particular business. Corporate public relations includes the publicity and promotional campaigns that increase awareness of the organization's products and services. Corporate publicity and promotional activities involve media relations, writing and distributing news releases, product placements, event planning, and other PR activities.

There are many additional components of a comprehensive corporate public relations program beyond publicity and promotional efforts. Additional aspects of corporate public relations involves: branding, crisis communication, managing the company's reputation and image, positioning the company as socially responsible, investor relations, and employee relations.

Corporate public relations professionals can be involved in all aspects of a company's communication efforts with its external and internal publics. Duties that often fall under the scope of corporate communications involve: writing or editing all print communication; speech writing; coordinating media interviews; coaching executives on interview techniques; preparing and designing annual reports; preparing, designing, and distributing employee newsletters; coordinating special events; organizing crisis communication efforts; recommending and promoting charitable donations and community activities; and many other tasks.

5| Fashion Public Relations Targets Consumers and Retail Decision Makers

Fashion public relations focuses on building brand awareness and a cultivating positive public image for all types of organizations within the fashion industry, including clothing designers, accessories designers, and fashion retailers. Successful fashion public relations involves a combination of strategic product placements and targeted print, broadcast, and online publicity. Contacts with fashion editors and writers (for trade and consumer publications and websites), broadcast producers, and celebrity stylists are very important in fashion public relations.

A major goal of fashion public relations efforts is to increase product and brand awareness within the target consumer population. Fashion public relations also targets decision makers within the fashion trade, specifically retail buyers and managers and the fashion merchandisers involved in creating visual displays within the retail outlets. Consumer awareness of products is only beneficial if the products are available to consumers, so a great deal of fashion PR focuses on the behind-the-scenes aspects of the fashion industry.

Many fashion businesses, both new and established, rely on public relations agencies who specialize in the fashion industry to handle their publicity. The contacts of an experienced fashion PR firm can be an invaluable resource for publicity and product placements within the highly competitive fashion industry.

6| How to Choose Among Public Relations Companies

There are many different public relations companies located all over the world, and it is a safe bet that a number of them would like to represent your organization. Choosing among public relations firms is a big task, and the decision about which company will handle your company's PR is an important one. There are a number of things you can do to make sure that you are making an informed decision.

The first thing that you should look for is a good rapport between you and the representative, usually called an Account Executive, who will be your primary contact with the public relations company. It is extremely important that you are comfortable with this person and communicate well with him or her.

It is also a good idea to ask to meet the other agency representatives who will be assigned to work on your account. Even though the Account Executive will likely be your primary contact, the other members of the account team will be representing your company to the news media as well as to members of the general public. It only makes sense to be sure that you are comfortable that each member of the team will represent your organization well if selected to handle your public relations.

Assuming that you are comfortable with the personnel you meet, you should ask to see examples of the firm's work and documentation of the results of these campaigns. If a public relations company can't provide results, this can be a sign either that their campaigns are not effective or that they do not bother to track the results of their campaigns. The most well-written news releases and attractive brochures are of no benefit to you if they don't generate results.

It is probably in your best interest to engage the services of a public relations firm that has experience in your industry. One of the primary advantages of using a PR company to handle your publicity is the media contacts that the firm already has. However, if you are in charge of PR for a hospital, and the firm you are considering only has experience in the fashion public relations, pre-existing media relationships that might benefit you are non-existent. You may be better served going with a firm that has a long track record of success in healthcare public relations.

You should also ask for client references. It is definitely a good idea to chat with a few of the firm's clients before you make a final decision. Clients can give you insight into how quickly the firm's reps return telephone calls, how open they are to client input, if the firm prices its work fairly, etc.

7| Planning a PR Campaign Involves Identifying Goals, Publics, Strategies and Tactics

A public relations campaign is systematic PR plan created for the purpose of achieving a particular goal or set of **goals**. In order to develop a public relations campaign, you need to first determine what goal you wish to accomplish. If you start putting together a PR campaign without a clearly defined goal, you may find yourself engaging in a lot of PR activities, but not making forward progress that will have any real benefit to your business.

To determine your goal, ask yourself what you really hope to accomplish as a result of the PR campaign. Are you launching a new product? If so, is your primary need to raise consumer awareness of the product, or do you also need to get it on the shelves in major retail outlets?

Once you know your goal, the next step in developing a public relations campaign is to **identify the target publics**. In PR, a "public" is any group who affects or is affected by your organization. Which groups need to be targeted for this particular campaign? You have to know who you are trying to reach in order to determine the best way to get your message to them.

When you know who your target publics are, you can begin creating public relations **strategies** and **tactics** that you will use to send your message. A strategy is a particular public relations technique, such as "generate -print media publicity for consumer market" and tactics are the specific actions that will be made to accomplish the strategy.

The process of identifying strategies requires brainstorming a list of the public relations techniques that will be most effective in accomplishing the overall goal of the campaign. Once you decide which strategies to pursue, the next step will be to make a list of every action that will be taken in support of that strategy.

Example :

Strategy : Generate Print Media Publicity for Consumer Market

Tactics :

- develop targeted consumer magazines media list
- develop targeted newspaper editor media list
- write "coming soon" news release
- distribute "coming soon news release"
- write "product launch" news release
- distribute "product launch" news release
- other relevant activities

Once you have identified your goal, target publics, strategies, and tactics, the next steps will be to create a timeline, and then get to work implementing your public relations campaign.

8| Provide Product and Service Information to Targeted Consumer Media

Consumer public relations efforts are among the most cost effective and efficient ways of sharing information about your company's products and services with the target audience. There are a number of online and offline publicity outlets that can be very effective for reaching a consumer audience.

The first thing you will need to do is generate a media list of editors and reporters who cover the types of products or services you provide in the consumer media. The consumer media can include radio, television, newspaper, magazine, blogs, ezines, newsletters, and any other type of print or electronic publication that consumers in your target audience use.

By writing effective news releases and submitting them to the consumer media via mail, email, fax, hand-delivery, or online press release distribution services, you can generate many different types of media coverage for your organization. If your company markets a tangible product, it can also be beneficial to provide samples of the product to members of the media who cover the industry.

For example, if your company is marketing a new cookbook or food product, it is a good idea to send a copy of the book or a sample of the food item to the food editors of major newspapers and the editors of food-oriented magazines and blogs. If it is a cookbook or food product for people with diabetes, you can also expand your media contacts to include health editors and magazines.

Spend time perusing the media outlets that your target audience uses so that you become familiar with the types of information that they are likely to cover. By making yourself knowledgeable about what types of things interest those who write for the consumer media that you are targeting, you can better position yourself to come up with and pitch story ideas that can generate coverage for your company.

9| Public Relations Agencies Provide Professional Consulting and Services

Public relations agencies can provide many different services to their clients. The extent of the services provided varies, based on the terms of the client agreement. In some cases, public relations agencies handle every aspect of a company's public relations activities and strategies. In other cases, public relations agencies strictly handle one or two PR functions, such as event planning or media relations.

The many different services offered by full-service public relations agencies include:

- Media Relations: maintaining an accurate media list, cultivating relationships with reporters and editors, handling inquiries from the news media

- Publicity: coming up with story angles, writing news releases and articles, submitting them to appropriate media and other distribution outlets, tracking coverage

- Community Relations: seeking out and coordinating opportunities to increase client visibility within the community (such as speaking engagements, board seats, etc.)

- Strategic Planning: Working with the company to develop an ongoing PR strategy that is in line with its overall organizational goals and objectives

- Crisis Communications: Developing a contingency plan and helping the company handle communications efforts in the event that a public relations crisis situation occurs

- Event Planning: Handling all aspects of setting up special events, such as ribbon cuttings, ground breakings, anniversary celebrations, employee recognition events, etc.

- Speech Writing: Writing speeches for company leaders

- Collateral Materials: Writing and designing documents such as company newsletters, annual plans, ezines, brochures, flyers, eBooks, whitepapers, etc.

- Additional types of promotional activities and consulting services.

10| A Good Lead Can Make or Break Your Press Release

Many reporters are bombarded with press releases on a daily basis, and they don't have time to read every word of every document they receive. Instead, they are likely to scan the many press releases they receive for ones that catch their attention. The very beginning, often called the **lead**, of your news release has to capture the interest of a journalist in order to make him or her want to read the entire document.

Being able to write a good lead is an important part of knowing how to write an effective press release. The headline and summary statements at the beginning of your news release have to speak to the reporter. They must convey what is newsworthy about the information presented in the document, and they must be written in a manner that convinces the reporter that his or her readers will be interested in and benefit from learning about it.

A great lead won't help you out if the rest of your press release is poorly written, formatted incorrectly, or lacks sufficient detail. However, without a great lead, chances are that the journalists who receive the news release won't even read the entire document.

11| Customize the Press Release Angle Based on the Audience

One of the most important press release how to guidelines is the importance of customizing press releases so that they meet the specific needs of the reporters who will receive them. For example, if your company is introducing a new, low-calorie food product that is made with organic ingredients and is marketed in biodegradable packaging, you can easily adjust the angle of a basic new product press release to appeal to several different types of journalists.

In this case, editors and writers who cover food, diet, nutrition, environmental issues, farming, and gardening may all be interested in learning about your new product. However, they won't all be interested for the same reasons. Customizing news releases based on the interests of the recipients is an important technique for maximizing media coverage.

To increase your chances of generating publicity, you can create a news release specific to each angle of the new product introduction by writing a unique headline and summary based on each newsworthy angle of the item. The body of the news release can generally stay the same, as long as the headline speaks directly to the type of publication or the interests of the reporter (environmental, food, diet, etc.) who receives it.

12| Good Press Releases Read Like News Stories

Writing for the media is very different from writing an advertisement, a brochure, an essay, or a research paper. Press releases must be written using a journalistic writing style rather than a creative one.

Even if you have never written for the news media, you have certainly read a number of news stories. A good press release reads like a news story. It is not simply a disguised advertisement for your company, and must not include sales-oriented language. News releases should be written in a concise manner, with brief sentences and short paragraphs.

A press release that is likely to result in publicity is one that is written from an objective, third-person perspective. The information presented must be factual and verifiable and should provide the reporter with relevant details that address the who, what, where, when, why, and how of the story.

13| Make Sure Information is Newsworthy Before Writing a Press Release

One of the secrets of successful press release writing is to understand the criteria for newsworthiness. For information to be considered newsworthy, you need to be able to answer "yes" to at least one of the following questions about the story or information you are trying to pitch:

- Is it **timely** ? (i.e., Does it tie to current events? Has it occurred recently or is it about to happen?)

- Does the information have an element of **proximity** ? (i.e., Does it "hit close to home?")

- Is **relevant** to the journalist's audience?

- Does it have the potential to **impact** the audience?

- Is there an element of **conflict** ?

- Is the information **fresh** ?

- Is there something **unusual** about the story?

- Is it easy to identify how the **audience will benefit** from receiving the information?

- Does the story present an **innovation** ?

- Is a **prominent** figure or organization involved in the story?

Answering "yes" to one or more of these questions is not a guarantee that your story will be considered newsworthy to a particular reporter. Without these elements, it's unlikely that anyone will find your story to be newsworthy.

14| Proper Grammar is a Must in Press Release Writing

No matter what type of document you are writing on behalf of your company, using proper grammar is always important. People often form opinions, consciously and subconsciously, about the quality of companies and their employees based on the accuracy and style accuracy and style of the written documentation used.

When you are writing press releases, you are creating written documents for the specific purpose of sending them to journalists, who are professional writers. More so than anyone else who receives correspondence from your company, reporters are likely to quickly notice and be influenced by grammatical errors.

If you send out press releases with grammatical errors, the reporters who receive them might question the accuracy and the information itself. Poorly written content can easily raise questions about information credibility. It is easy to assume that someone who doesn't check their writing for grammatical errors before sending it out might not have thoroughly checked out all the facts in the document. Since journalists are held to high standards of reporting accuracy, if they doubt your credibility, they aren't likely to use your press releases as a starting point for stories.

15| There is No Place for Puffery in Press Releases

One of the most important press release writing tips is to avoid using what journalists refer to as "puffery". Examples of puffery include statements such as: "XYZ company is the all-time favorite" or "XYZ widget is the best in the world." These are statements of opinion; they are not verifiable objective facts.

Journalists will not use press releases that are written using editorialized, sales-y language. If a press release reads more like advertising copy than like a news story, it isn't going to appeal to a reporter, which means that it isn't going to generate publicity for your company.

Save the comments about how great your company's products and services are for your advertising messages and sales pitches. When it comes to writing news releases, stick to the facts at all times.

16| Think Like a Journalist to Write Effective Press Releases

To understand how to write an effective press release, you have to think like a journalist. While the ultimate goal might be to sell your product or service to consumers, that is not what interests a journalist. Journalists aren't in the business of promoting companies. They are responsible for provide factual, objective, and newsworthy information to their readers and viewers.

Before you actually start writing a press release, you need to stop and think about what it is about your product or service that will interest a journalist. While the features and benefits of what your company does may be fascinating to you, a journalist isn't likely to be as fascinated. Stay away from "sales-y" language in press releases.

Every press release you write should have an angle. They angle you choose has to be one that is newsworthy if you want a journalist to pick up the story. Don't focus on why people buy your products or services when you are trying to come up with an angle for a press release. Instead, think about how to interest a reporter in sharing information about your organization with his or her audience.

17| Use the Inverted Pyramid Writing Style to Write Press Releases

If part of your job is to write press releases, you need to learn to write using the inverted pyramid writing style. Most news stories follow this style, and members of the news media expect that press releases will also be written in this manner.

To understand the concept of the inverted pyramid, simply visualize an upside down triangle. The largest area is at the top, and the shape gradually decreases down to the smallest point at the bottom. When you write using the inverted pyramid writing style, your writing will follow this design. You will start with the most important information at the beginning, and you will conclude with the least important information.

When you are writing press releases, keep in mind that the entire document might not be published. Of course, there is always a chance that none of your press release will be printed. However, when news releases are printed, they are often not be used in their entirety. The best way to make sure that important details aren't left out is to put them at the top of the document. Typically, when partial news releases are published in the print media, the information at the end of the document is what is eliminated.

18| Write With Keywords for Powerful Press Releases

Because many press releases are being published online, either via online syndication, web-based press release distribution, on company websites, or in other ways, it is important to keep search engine optimization in mind when you write press releases.

Using keywords in your press releases can make them an even more powerful marketing tool for your business than if you submit them without keywords. By including carefully selected keywords in your press releases, you can increase the likelihood that the documents will be found by people who are searching for the types of products or services that you offer.

For example, having keywords in your press releases can make it easier for journalists who subscribe to online news release distribution services to find your company when looking for specific types of information related to its products and services. Additionally, with so many opportunities to distribute and publish press releases online, these documents can actually become powerful tools for reaching end-use consumers whether or not they are picked up for use in traditional media outlets.

Press Release
Submission

19| Benefits of Paid Press Release Distribution

There are advantages to using a paid press release distribution service or newswire to submit your press releases. Paid distribution services typically offer a number of benefits over the free services, particularly if you are submitting time sensitive information and you want to increase the chances of having your news release picked up by a major media outlet.

Benefits of Paid Press Release Distribution

- Ability to add multimedia content
- Distribution options (regional, particular types of media, industry-specific distribution, etc.)
- Media credibility
- Press release editing services
- Same day distribution
- Social media bookmark links

Some of the most popular paid press release distribution services are:

- prweb.com
- prnewswire.com

20| Consider Reporter Preferences When Submitting a Press Release

When deciding how to submit a press release to the media, you have to consider the preferences of the journalists you are targeting. Many newspaper and television outlets prefer to receive press releases via major newswire services. However, some journalists, producers, and editors like to receive press releases via email. Many monthly magazines do not subscribe to newswire services and so will often not find out about your news releases if you do not email or fax them to the editor.

If you are planning to submit press releases to media outlets in your local community or region on a regular basis, it is a good idea for you to take the time to get to know the media professionals that you are targeting. This will help you start to cultivate a positive relationship with them, and also allow you to find out how they prefer to receive news releases.

Keep in mind that the best way to submit news releases to a media professional is whatever way he or she prefers to receive them!

21| Determining the Best Time to Submit a Press Release

There is no hard and fast rule regarding the best time to submit a press release. If you are dealing with time-sensitive information, the best time to submit your press release is immediately, while it is still newsworthy. However, if you are submitting a press release that doesn't have a sense of urgency associated with current events, you should try schedule the submission of your press release on days that are likely to be least hectic for the journalists who will receive them.

For example, if you are planning to submit your press release to daily print or broadcast media outlets (directly or via a newswire service), keep in mind that reporters are likely to be overwhelmed with press releases on Friday and Monday. Many PR professionals feel that Wednesdays tend to be the best day for newswire submission for non-urgent press releases. You also have to consider media outlet deadlines. If you are submitting a press release that you hope will run in your local newspaper's Sunday Business section, be sure to get it to the appropriate journalist well in advance of the deadline.

It can be hard to predict which days might become hectic due to a significant news event. Sometimes a major story will break on a day that is typically a slow news day. If a major event happens at the same time you have planned to submit a press release to the media, you may want to delay submitting it. If it has already gone, realize that coverage might take a back seat to pressing news events.

22| Increase Press Release Exposure with Online Classified Advertising Sites

When you really want to maximize the benefits of submitting press releases online, you need to think outside the box. Of course, it is beneficial to submit your press releases to the many different free online press release websites and submission services. However, don't stop there when you really want to maximize publicity.

There are numerous online classified advertising sites that accept free advertisements. While some of these sites are designed specifically to sell products from one individual to another, many of them are ideal places to post your company's news releases.

A few of the free classified advertising sites that can help maximize press release exposure are:

- adlandpro.com
- craigslist.org
- domesticsale.com
- usfreeads.com

Keep in mind that you should read and comply with the terms of any free classified advertising site that you use to distribute your press releases.

23| Objective and Content Determines Where to Submit Press Releases

There are many different places to submit press releases. Selecting the best places to submit your press releases depends on your objective and the content of the documents. If you are concerned with building backlinks for your website, it is to your advantage to submit releases to the many different free press release websites and newswires.

However, if you hope that your press release might result in an appearance on a talk show or a feature story in a newspaper or magazine, you need to send press releases to journalists, editors, and producers who might be interested in the topic. Do not assume that reporters will see your news releases posted on free news release websites. Consumers might see them, but it is very likely that reporters will not. When you need to get information to media professionals, you should utilize the services of a major newswire service or use your own media list to make sure that you are able to submit press releases directly to the right people.

When preparing to submit releases, think about which media outlets and journalists might actually be interested in what you have to say. If you are launching a new restaurant in your community, you should definitely send a press release to the food editor. If the restaurant has a sports theme, you may want send your news business announcement to the sports editor as well. However, the editor of the gardening section isn't likely to be interested. Don't bother reporters with information that isn't related to their beats, but make sure that you do send releases to every editorial department that might legitimately be interested in the topic.

24| Proofread Press Releases Carefully Before Submitting

Before you submit your press release to the media or post it online, proofread it very carefully to make sure that it conveys the right message. Verify that the content is accurate and well-written, and check the document for typographical errors and spelling mistakes. Make sure that it is properly formatted and written in the appropriate inverted pyramid writing style.

When you submit press releases, or engage in any other public relations activities, one of your objectives is to sustain or created a positive impact on your organization's image. If you send documents to the news media, or publish them online, and they are poorly written or full of errors, your efforts will backfire. Instead of helping your company's image, press releases that are have not been properly proofed and edited will actually hurt it.

25| The New Rules of When to Submit Press Releases

Before the Internet evolved into the Web 2.0 communication tool it has become today, the best time to submit a press release was when a truly monumental, newsworthy event occurred. Press releases were distributed only to members of the news media, who decided whether or not the information would ever be passed along to the public. Of course, newsworthy press releases can and should still be submitted to journalists. Traditional publicity is still a very important component of any corporate communications plan.

However, press releases can be used for many additional purposes today. Companies can now use press releases to communicate directly with consumers any time they choose to do so. Businesses can post press releases on their own websites, and optimize them so they can easily be found by consumers. They can be distributed to subscribers via ezine newsletters. Press releases can also be submitted to many free online press release websites and distribution services, where they can be seen by consumers and play an important role in optimizing the organization's website by creating backlinks.

Companies who are fully utilizing the power of press releases as a direct-to-consumer communications tool write and submit press releases on a regular basis. They have become an important tool for both search engine optimization and for keeping the company's name in front of consumers

26| Where to Submit Press Releases for Free Exposure and SEO

There are many different free press release websites and distribution services. Taking the time to submit your press releases to these sites can be very beneficial for two reasons. First, the backlinks created when your press releases post to these sites can improve your website's search engine ranking. Second, consumers and even media professionals may find your news releases through these services.

Some free press release distribution sites are:

- 888pressrelease.com
- newsblaze.com
- pr9.net
- prfree.com
- sanepr.com
- theopenpress.com

Make sure that you read and comply with the terms of any free press release service that you utilize.

27| Associated Press Newswire: 24/7 News Updates From Around the World

Thousands of media organizations rely on the Associated Press newswire for around the clock news updates from every corner of the globe. The organization has approximately 3,000 reporters on staff and operates 243 bureaus in 97 countries. AP prides itself on delivering timely, objective, reliable, and accurate news information to its customers, including newspapers, radio stations, television stations, and online subscribers such as the Dow Jones newswire and numerous other high visibility services.

28| Benefits of Free Newswire Services

There are a number of free newswire services that accept press releases for distribution to a variety of media and new media outlets. Most of the free newswire services offer both basic-level no-cost distribution options and enhanced paid distribution options.

If your primary goal for distributing press releases is to attract the attention of journalists at major media outlets, you may benefit from to use one of the major subscription-based newswire services instead of or in addition to free newswire services. However, if you are distributing press releases to enhance your company's online visibility and search engine ranking via search engine optimization, utilizing free newswire services can be a very beneficial publicity tactic.

Some free newswire distribution services include:

- Newswire Today (general newswire)

- PR Zoom (business news wire)

- The Open Press (general newswire)

- Entertainment Wire Service (entertainment and music newswire)

29| Business Wire: Full-Text Industry and Financial News Release Distribution

Business Wire provides worldwide news release distribution services for business entities. On behalf of its members, Business Wire transmits critical regulatory filings, full-text press releases, photographs, and other types of multimedia content to targeted editorial contacts, regulatory agencies, stock exchanges, financial analysts and investors, and the general public.

Business Wire's newswire distribution system sends member information via a network of approximately 60 news agencies, financial service providers, and Internet-based news wires around the world. The Business Wire network encompasses over 150 industries. News release distribution can be tailored for specific industries, and can also be targeted to a geographic are as narrow as one city or as broad as the network reaches.

For publicly trades companies who must comply with Securities and Exchange Commission's EDGAR document filing regulations, Business Wire's offers a unique regulatory compliance service that combines financial newswire distribution of press releases with filing mandatory forms.

For information on becoming a Business Wire member, call 1-888-381-WIRE.

30| Canadian Newswire Services Provide Electronic News Release Distribution

One of the most efficient ways to distribute information to media outlets across Canada is by using a Canadian newswire service. Public relations practitioners who need to distribute news releases and other information to media outlets frequently rely on the services of the CNW Group, the largest and most recognized news wire service in Canada.

The CNW Group operates seven news bureaus across Canada, with offices in Calgary, Halifax, Montreal, Ottawa, Quebec City, Toronto, and Vancouver. Client organizations can submit press releases directly through their local bureaus. The newswire is updated around the clock, and is distributed electronically to newsrooms and financial market contacts throughout the country. Additionally, client news releases are posted on the CNW Group's website, which is Canada's highest traffic full text online resource for news releases.

In addition to traditional newswire services, the CNW group also assists clients with a variety of communications needs, including audio and video webcasting services that allow them to broadcast information on a worldwide basis in real time.

Information on using the CNW Group's Canadian newswire services can be found at www.newswire.ca.

31| Christian Newswire Delivers Religious News Directly to Targeted Media Contacts

ChristianNewswire.com is a paid news release distribution service that distributes religious news releases directly to reporters at major new media, broadcast and print media outlets around the world. For example, Christian Newswire feeds go to the appropriate contacts all of the major search engines, daily newspapers, the AP newswire, a Hispanic newswire (Hispanic Link News Service), medical newswires, top radio and television talk show hosts, and many others. Additionally, interested individuals can register on the website to receive news releases via e-mail. Public relations practitioners who utilize Christian Newswire distribution can select specific distribution options based on geography, type of media, and type of information covered. Specific beat distributions include: conservative/pro-family, Catholic media, opinion editors, black media, and others.

32| How to Submit News Releases to AP Newswire

The best way to submit a news release to the AP newswire depends on the scope and nature of the information. Associated Press does not publish individual email addresses or contact numbers for its editorial staff members, but does provide detailed instructions for submitting press releases to ensure that they are forwarded to the appropriate parties.

News releases of national or international significance can be e-mailed, in the body of an e-mail message, to info@ap.org. They can also be mailed to the following address:

450 West 33rd Street
New York, NY, 10001

Address national news releases to "AP General/National Desk" and international information should be addressed to "International Desk at Associated Press." News releases related to stories of regional or local significance should be sent to the appropriate local AP news bureau office. Telephone numbers, fax numbers, and addresses for each state's bureau can be found on the "Contact Us" page of www.ap.org.

Additionally, the names of editors and writers who cover specific beats for Associated Press newswire (arts and entertainment, business news, lifestyles, news features, and sports) can also be found on the "Contact Us" page.

33| Market Wire: Customized News Release Distribution for U.S. and Canada

Market Wire is a subscription based service that helps public relations practitioners manage and target their news release distribution. Market Wire's clients are able to access the organization's comprehensive database of media contacts to create their own targeted contact lists for print, broadcast, newswire services, online information services, and new media outlets. Market Wire's centralized database system makes sure that contact information is current at all times. Additionally Market Wire has exclusive access to The Canadian Press Wire Network, a Canadian newswire service.

When distributing news releases through Market Wire, clients are able to enhance their documents with multimedia features such as video, photographs, sound, and other options. Media distribution lists can be customized in a number of ways, including state, region, industry, and special interest.

Market Wire also assists clients effectively manage the flow of their press release distribution efforts and track the results. The organization monitors newswire services, new media services, financial information services, and other resources to help clients keep track of where their releases post and where their organization is mentioned.

34| PR Newswire: Targeted Electronic News Release Distribution

PR Newswire is a subscription-based electronic news release distribution service. Client news releases are distributed to news media, financial and governmental decision-makers, and the general public. With around the clock content delivery, many media professionals rely on PR Newswire for around the clock updates on breaking news, direct from the source.

Thousands of media outlets around the world receive PR newswire updates via satellite, and many more receive updates via email and facsimile delivery. Additionally, more than 80,000 journalists have registered for access to the company's journalist-specific website, where client news releases are posted. PR Newswire also operates websites that allow clients to make full-text news releases available to other decision makers and consumers.

PR Newswire subscribers can send news releases across the entire news wire service, or select geographic or industry targeted distribution. PR newswire offers a number of additional services that can support corporate communications objectives such as video news releases, evaluation and measurement, and targeting.

Information on utilizing PR Newswire's services can be found at www.prnewswire.com.

35| Include the Correct Contacts on Your Media List

- Section editors at daily newspapers (For example, information about business books goes to business editors, information about new cookbooks goes to food editors, etc.)

- Producers for television and radio talk shows that reach the book's target audience

- Bloggers who write about topics of interest to the target population

- Online press release posting and distribution websites

- Publishers of newsletters and e-zines that reach the target market.

36| Asian Media Outlets Get Messages to Asian American Population

The Asian American population is expanding rapidly, and media outlets that cater to their needs are increasing and expanding. New publications that target the Asian American population are coming into existence, and mainstream media are expanding coverage of issues relevant to this market segment.

The Gebbie Press (www.gebbieinc.com) All-In-One Media directory can be a valuable tool for creating a contact list of journalists at Asian Media outlets, as well as many other types of media outlets. The US Asian Newswire (www.usasianwire.com) provides PR practitioners with the ability to distribute news releases to the ever increasing list of Asian American media outlets and to reach mainstream media representatives interested in and sensitive to the needs of this population.

Examples of Asian American Publications

Asian American Times - This bilingual Chinese-English newspaper emphasizes stories of interest to immigrants, such as information about U.S. rules, laws, and politics. Updates on current events in Asia are often included. The semi-monthly subscription based publication can be found online at (www.asiantimes.com).

Asian Week - This publication serves the growing United States population of Asians and Pacific Islanders. It is the oldest and largest English language newspaper targeting this segment of the United States population. In addition to the print publication, www.AsianWeek.com is a leading English-language news site focused specifically on America's Asian and Pacific Islander community.

37| Black Media Outlets Effective for Reaching African American Community

There are many different African American newspapers, magazines, radio stations and talk shows, and television stations throughout the United States. Black media outlets typically cover issues about and of interest to the African American community.

Resources for Black Media Outlets:

- Black News (www.blacknews.com): new media, daily online news site

- Black Press USA (www.blackpressusa.com): online community of black newspapers

- Gebbie Press All-In-One Directory (www.gebbieinc.com): general media directory with listings of black newspapers, magazines, and radio stations

- Radio Black (www.radioblack.com): worldwide directory of radio stations catering to Black, urban, and African American populations

Newswire Distribution Specific to Black Media Outlets:

- Black Media Newswire (www.blackmedianewswire.com)

- Black Newswire (www.blacknewswire.com)

- Black PR (www.blackpr.com)

38| How to Build Relationships with Journalists

By taking the time to build relationships with journalists, you increase the likelihood that they will (a) help your press releases find their way to the top of the pile, (b) take phone calls from you, (c) refer you to other reporters and (d) call you when they need a source or a quote.

Tips for Building Relationships with Journalists:

- **Network with reporters.** Get involved in your local Society of Professional Journalists chapter. Don't just attend meetings; really get involved. By working on committees, you will build invaluable relationships with the news media in your local community.

- **Be trustworthy.** Do what you say when you say you will do it, and always be honest. If you ever lie to a reporter or give a reporter misleading information, the relationship will be permanently damaged.

- **Be respectful.** Always treat reporters with courtesy and respect. Do not ever suggest or imply that a reporter "owes" you coverage.

- **Adhere to Code of Ethics.** Don't put reporters in uncomfortable positions by offering to pay for coverage in any way shape or form. Be aware of the ethical standards followed by journalists.

- **Don't be a fair weather contact.** Maintain relationships and contact with reporters.

- **Be considerate of deadlines.** Good PR practitioners learn the deadlines that their media contacts work under and time communications so they do not delay reporters.

39| How to Find Christian Media Outlets

Most cities have at least one Christian radio station and weekly newspaper publication, and most daily newspapers have a religion editor. There are also a number of national publications dedicated to the interests of Christians. Developing relationships with editors and reporters at Christian media outlets is very important for PR practitioners who hope to generate publicity that will reach the Christian population. One of the best resources for distributing press releases to a large number of Christian media outlets and reporters in the mainstream media who cover issues related to Christianity is the Christian Newswire (www.christiannewswire.com). This service has been operating since 1989, and is recognized as the leading U.S. distributor of religious content press releases.

Examples of Christian Media Outlets:

- Catholic Newspapers Directory (www.catholicnewspapers.com): Contact information for local, regional, national, and international Catholic newspapers.

- Christian Century (www.christiancentury.org): Semi-monthly magazine designed to nurture faith that covers issues of politics, culture, and theology.

- Christianity Today (www.christianitytoday.com): National magazine focused on evangelical conviction.

- National Catholic Register (www.ncregister.com): National newspaper targeting Catholic population

40| Improve Media Coverage Success with Customized Pitches

Before you pitch stories to reporters, its important to know something about the media outlets they represent. There are many different types of media outlets, each of which has a particular style and reaches certain segments of the population. The same pitch won't work with all types of media outlets, because different types have different needs.

There are many ways to research media outlets before pitching stories to them. The best PR practitioners understand the importance of getting familiar with the publications, programs, and websites where they hope to be covered. Editors and reporters are interested in stories that appeal to their readers. You need to know something about the types of stories they cover in order to come up with the best angle to pitch for your story.

If you are hoping to get a story published in XYZ magazine or on GBR blog, read and study the publication before you contact the editor. If you hope to book an appearance on a talk show, watch it over a period of time to develop an understanding of the program's booking preferences. If you contact every reporter with a generic pitch, you are likely to strike out more often than not. By getting to know the audience, style, and needs of individual media outlets and then customizing your pitch for each outlet, you can greatly improve your media coverage success rate.

41| Reach Growing Latino Market Segment Through Hispanic Media Outlets

The Hispanic population has an enormous economic impact in the United States and around the world. More and more companies are developing marketing campaigns designed specifically to target this growing population. Members of the Hispanic population tend to remain very emotionally attached to their home countries, and so seek out media that help them stay connected. Hispanic media outlets are viewed very favorably within the Latino community, and companies that are covered in them are often perceived as being very credible.

Spanish language writing and speaking skills are of utmost importance when seeking PR within the Latino community. PR practitioners who wish to target Hispanic Media outlets must develop press releases and pitches specifically for the Latino market. More and more Hispanic media outlets are opening in the United States as the population continues to grow. Hispanic Media (www.hispanic-media.com) is a valuable resource for current media contact information.

The Hispanic PR Wire (www.hispanicprwire.com) is a powerful tool for distributing news releases to influencers in the Hispanic community. This service reaches journalists, organizations, elected officials, and other opinion leaders within the Latino community throughout the United States. News releases can be distributed across the full wire, or targeted by category and/or region.

The Hispanic Market Weekly (www.hispanicmarketweekly.com) newsletter is a valuable resource for PR practitioners interested in learning more about the best ways to reach Hispanic consumers. In addition to receiving valuable tips in the weekly publication, subscribers have access to data and contact information for Hispanic media outlets in the United States, including magazines, newspapers, radio stations, and television stations.

42| Resources for Building News Media Contact Lists

A good media relations plan must incorporate strategies and tactics for getting information in front of the right editorial staffers at news media outlets that reach your target audience at the right time. News media outlets include any and all organizations that consumers rely upon for news and information about current events. Generating news media coverage requires getting to know who covers the types of events that affect or are affected by your organization in all types of media outlets. One of the most important tools any PR practitioner can have is a solid contact list of reporters, editors, staff writers, producers, etc., at all types media outlets who are potential sources of media coverage. Newswire services can also be very beneficial for disseminating news releases in a timely and effective manner.

Types of news media outlets:

Print - newspaper, magazines, newsletters

Broadcast - radio, television

New Media - news search engines, online news sites, blogs, podcasts, etc.

Resources for Media Contact Information:

- Bacon's Media Directories (www.us.cision.com)
- Gebbie Press All-In-One Directory (www.gebbieinc.com)
- Media Post (www.mediapost.com)
- Mondo Times (www.mondotimes.com)

Leading Newswire Services Include:

- PR Newswire (www.prnewswire.com)
- PR Web Direct (www.prwebdirect.com)

43| Timeless Public Relations Techniques

The public relations industry has greatly changed since *Confessions of a PR Man* was first published in 1988. However, the theory behind why public relations works and the principles of developing a sound media relations strategy haven't changed. This book is a must-read for anyone who hopes to succeed long-term in the public relations industry.

To really excel as a public relations practitioner in today's world, you certainly have to embrace the new technologies. It's also important to understand the history of PR and the basic premises of sound PR practice to be able to create and manage public campaigns that work, whether they involve traditional media, new media, or even non-media promotions.

Confessions of a PR Man provides highlights from Robert Woods' varied and successful career in public relations spanning more than four decades. Readers will be entertained, educated, and inspired by the unique examples of PR in action. If you really want to master the arts of image and issues management, generating publicity, influencing public opinion, and crisis communication, reading this book will be one of the most valuable things you have ever done.

44| What is Media Relations?

Many people perceive media relations as being nothing more than schmoozing reporters over long lunches and hosting media events. Fun!

While it is true that media relations may occasionally involve these things, an effective media relations strategy involves much more than the types of things you see PR practitioners doing in the movies.

What is Media Relations?

Media relations involves identifying and cultivating relationships with members of the news media who have the ability to influence public opinion about your company's products, services, or the industry in which it operates.

Effective Media Relations Strategies Include:

- Maintaining a current media contact list

- Being a trustworthy source of information

- Getting to know reporters who cover your beat

- Going out of your way to help reporters and editors get information they need

- Making yourself easily accessible to editorial contacts

- Sending only relevant, valuable information to reporters

- Treating editorial contacts with respect at all times

- Never asking a reporter to compromise the standards of journalistic ethics

- Being involved in the media community

- Expressing appreciation to reporters for fair coverage

- Always being forthright in communication with reporters

- Educating company executives and clients on proper media communication skills and etiquette

45| Benefits of Optimized Press Release Distribution

Writing and distributing optimized press releases can be the least expensive and most effective means of maximizing your company's exposure to the media and to prospective consumers. Optimized press release distribution can play important roles in both increasing awareness of your company and search engine optimization. The more places information about your company is published, offline and online, the more familiar consumers will become with your organization.

Optimized SEO Press Releases Can:

- Generate media coverage as a result of distribution to journalists

- Serve as fresh content on the company's website

- Be published in company blogs

- Generate buzz through submission to social networking websites

- Become permanent content on the company's website

- Create backlinks when press releases containing links to your website are published on other sites

- Have an overall positive impact on search engine optimization

- Be found online by people searching for utilized keyword phrases

- Drive organic traffic to the company's website

- Increase name recognition/brand awareness for the company

46| Enhance Media Coverage Opportunities by Publishing Press Releases on Your Own Website

If a reporter is looking for information about your company, he or she is likely to visit your website before doing any additional research. When a reporter can find needed information on your site right away, it saves time and trouble. This helps ensure that the deadline won't be missed and increases the chance that the reporter will probably return to your website when looking for sources or other information related to your field or industry.. It also increases the likelihood that the reporter will probably come back to your website again when looking for sources or other information related to your field or industry. By making it easy for reporters to find what they need without having to dig, you can really start to build long-term mutually beneficial relationships with journalists who cover beats related to your organization.

It doesn't cost anything to publish news releases on your own website, so there is no reason not to do it. There are many benefits to self-publishing your SEO news releases online. One of the primary benefits is the positive impact it can have on your ability to quickly provide reporters with information they need about your company, resulting in increased publicity for your business.

47| How SEO Press Releases Differ from Traditional Press Releases

Before search engine optimization became an important marketing consideration, press releases were written solely for journalists. Before the concept of Internet marketing changed the way that media outlets function and how companies promote their businesses, press releases were distributed very infrequently. Reporters would only consider using a news release that contained information about a very newsworthy event, and PR practitioners didn't want to risk annoying journalists by sending information likely to be deemed not worthy of publication.

In those days, the opportunity to get information about your organization in front of consumers was very limited. There are only so many minutes in a news broadcast and only so many pages in print publications. Occasionally a PR person would get lucky with a human interest or even filler story, but it certainly was not an everyday occurrence.

However, as the Internet began to grow in popularity, and marketing and public relations gurus began to realize its potential as a promotional tool, press release distribution evolved into something different entirely. Whereas once only major media outlets could make information readily accessible to the general public, now anyone with a website and some bandwidth is, in essence, a publisher.

Companies with their own websites can now publish their own press releases, which consumers can view and access at will. They can distribute them to other websites that publish and/or distribute press releases. They can visit blogs and forums and post information about their companies and organizations. In other words, press releases have become a direct-to-consumer communication tool in addition to a tool limited to being distributed to the news media.

By using keyword optimization techniques, PR practitioners are even able to exert some level of control over which types of consumers are likely to find their press releases online. Whereas traditional press releases were primarily intended for distribution to the public via the mass media, SEO press releases are a much more personalized form of targeted, direct-to consumer communication.

48| How to Create Search Engine Optimized Press Releases

When writing an effective SEO (search engine optimized) press release, many factors must be taken into consideration. It is very important to identify the keyword phrases that people are likely to use when searching for the type of content you are publishing, and incorporate them into both the title and the content of the document.

The proper use of keywords allows a news release published online to be found by users searching for similar content. A keyword selection tool, such as Overture (www.inventory.overture.com), can help you determine which phrases to use. SEO press releases also have to be an appropriate length, well-written, interesting, and appealing to journalists and consumers alike.

Optimized Press Release Do's:

- Conduct research to determine critical keyword phrases

- Begin headline with primary keyword phrase

- Include primary and additional keyword phrases in body of press release

- Ideal length is between 400 and 500 words

- Write an appealing headline

- Start with the most important information

- Cover the who, what, where, why and how

- Include a link to your website

49| How to Write a Good Title for an SEO Press Release

The body of your press release is very important. The title, however, may be even more important. The title of a press release serves two very important purposes. Regardless of whether the press release is published offline or online, the title has to be attention getting enough to catch and hold the reader's attention. When writing an SEO press release, the title serves an additional function. A well written title can ensure that your press release is indexed by search engines, thereby becoming easy to find online.

A good press release title includes the primary keyword phrase. The keyword phrase included in the title needs to be the one that people who are searching for similar content are most likely to use. By including your keyword phrase in the title, this phrase becomes the very first thing the search engine spiders pick up from the document. This increases the likelihood that you will be found near the top of the search engine results for your primary search terms.

A good SEO press release title alone isn't enough to guarantee you a top spot in the desired search engine results. However, it is the first step to getting the positioning you want. Without a title written in accordance with keyword optimization guidelines, no matter what else you write in the body of your press release, the document isn't going to index as high as you would like.

50| Keyword Optimization Attracts Attention from Journalists and Consumers

Press release optimization is the practice of writing and distributing high quality press releases that can lead to media coverage, inclusion in RSS news feeds to highly trafficked websites, continual publication of fresh online content about your organization, and improved search engine ranking for your company's website.

In order to enjoy the full benefits of online public relations, you must consider keyword optimization when selecting the title of your news release and when composing the content. The news release must be interesting, well-written, and really speak to the needs and interests of the target readers.

Keywords and keyword phrases should be selected based on frequency of searches and competition for indexing attention. Make sure that the keywords you incorporate into your press releases are, in fact, common search phrases used by people seeking the kind of products or services that your company has to offer. The only way that press releases can help drive organic traffic to your website is if they are indexed when Internet users are conducting online searches for similar products or services.

Proper use of critical keywords in your news releases ensures that they will attract the interest of journalists in these topics. The best SEO news release will not be of any benefit if it doesn't get to the right people at the right time. It is vital that your release be written in a manner that allows it to be easily found as the result of a relevant keyword search.

51| Keyword Optimization for Visibility in News Search Engines

One of the primary benefits of distributing optimized press releases via a newswire service is the ability to get indexed in one of the major news search engines, such as Google News (www.news.google.com), Yahoo! News (www.news.yahoo.com), and others. Millions of people, including journalists and consumers, rely on the top news search engines for up-to-the minute news on a daily basis. Consumers use news search engines for quick and easy access to the news stories they want to read about. Journalists often use them to locate potential interview subjects, get story ideas, and even to find filler for slow news days.

News search engines don't search the entire Internet for content. Instead, each search engine has its own list of "trusted news source sites" which it crawls for content, which is then ranked via the search engine's algorithm. Google News crawls more than 4,000 sources each day for news, and Yahoo News has more than 6,000 sources on its site. For your press releases to have any chance of being seen by a news search engine, they first have to be published on one of the trusted sites.

However, just being where Google News, Yahoo! News, or one of the other news search engines, can find you doesn't mean that reporters or consumers will ever find you in the news search engine. News search engine users search for desired content with keywords and keyword phrases, in exactly the same manner as anyone would search a general search engine. This is why press release optimization is so important. If you want to be found online, your content has to include critical keyword phrases.

When reporters or consumers locate your company's press release through news search engines, you can be certain that your information is getting in front of people who are likely to be actively looking for information related to the content of your news release. Additionally, there is a credibility boost associated with being located via a news search engine rather than through an advertisement or other type of online search.

Structuring and distributing your press releases so that they are likely to be indexed in news search engines is a powerful internet marketing strategy for increasing organic website traffic, generating media coverage, and making a positive impact on your bottom line.

52| Press Release Optimization Don'ts

Remember that when you distribute press releases, there is no guarantee that they will be published. You can, of course, choose to publish all your press releases on your own website. However, no one else has to publish them. When writing and distributing press releases, take care to ensure that the documents you are creating are interesting, well-written, and likely to appeal to consumers and journalists alike. Optimized press releases are only beneficial if they get published.

Press Release Don'ts:

- Do not send out press releases with grammatical, spelling, or typographical errors.

- Do not use a misleading title. Make sure that the title of your press release reflects the content of the document.

- Don't write the press release as if it were an advertisement. Statements of opinion, sales-oriented statements, exaggerated claims, etc. do not belong in a press release.

- Do not write in first person. (No "my company," "I am offering," etc.)

- Don't forget to add a link to your website in the body of the news release.

- Do not include an email address for publication unless you are perfectly fine knowing that it is going to be added to plenty of SPAM lists as soon as the press release is published.

53| Write Press Releases with Keyword Optimization in Mind

When writing press releases for online distribution, search engine optimization is of utmost importance. To enjoy the maximum promotional benefit of writing and publishing online press releases, you have created documents that the search engines are likely to see and index favorably. The same principles of search engine optimization (SEO) that apply to writing website content also apply to writing press releases.

A good SEO press release has to be written so that it appeals to consumers, journalists, and search engines. In order to be effective, press releases must be well-written and contain interesting content. They should start off with an attention-grabbing headline, and explain the who, what, where, why, when, and how most important to the topic. The language that is used must be easy-to-understand by people and by search engines.

If you want your press releases to help customers and prospective customers find your website as a result of search engine inquiries, you must write with keyword optimization in mind. You have to include the words or phrases that people who are looking for what you have to offer are likely to use when conducting Internet searches for similar products and services. The key to press release optimization is to incorporate everything you know about writing for the media with everything you know about how to write web content. The end result will be an effective public relations effort that drives organic traffic to your website.

54| How to Track Media Coverage Resulting from News Release Distribution

There are several different ways to track the types and quantity of media coverage resulting from news release distribution. Depending on how frequently you submit press releases, how widely you distribute them, and how exact your tracking needs to be, you might be able to track coverage yourself or you may need to utilize a clipping service.

News releases submitted online primarily for the purpose of search engine optimization can be tracked with some degree of certainty with the Google Alerts Tool (www.google.com/alerts). Simply register relevant keywords with the service, and you will receive email notices when Google indexes new top 50 results for the specified search terms.

Offline media coverage can be tricky to track. To verify coverage in the mass media, you either have to check through the publications yourself or contract a clipping service to do it for you. When dealing with widespread press release distribution, the assistance of a clipping service can be invaluable. Some of the best are: Burrells*Luce* (www.burrellesluce.com), Cyber Alert (www.cyberalert.com), and Cision (http://us.cision.com).

Do not ever ask a journalist to send you a clipping of your press release or story. Ever.

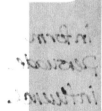

55| How to Write News Releases that Get Results

News release writing requires both writing skill and marketing savvy.

The writing skills involved include: proper grammar, spelling, and punctuation; using the inverted pyramid writing style; following AP Stylebook standards, and being able to clearly and concisely communicate the who, what, where, when, why, and how of the story.

In terms of marketing strategy, PR practitioners must be able to (a) sell reporters on covering the story and (b) understand what would interest prospective customers in the product or service. Get the results you want by answering the following questions when writing news releases for the media:

inform
persuade
influence

- What is the ultimate goal of your news release?

- Why is the target audience for your news release?

- How can I make this news release appeal to reporters?

- What is newsworthy about this story?

- What is unique about the story?

- Is there anything unusual about the story?

- Is there a way to tie the story in to current events?

- Should I write several news releases with different angles to appeal to reporters covering a variety of beats?

- Am I sending it to the right people?

- What is the best way to distribute this news release?

56| Invite Journalists to Cover Events with Media Alerts

The Media Alert is the best news release format to use when inviting journalists to an event. When holding an event that you would like members of the media to attend, send a media alert instead of a full-blown news release. Media alerts are typically used to invite media representatives to attend press conferences, ground breakings, grand openings, charitable donation ceremonies, and other types of events.

Media Alerts are brief, memo-style documents that state where and when an event will be held and pitches journalists on why they should cover it. They are typically sent to print and broadcast assignment editors and beat reporters who make decisions regarding which events will and will not be covered. They are typically sent via fax or email.

Media Alert Format Checklist:

- Contact information

- Release statement (For Immediate Release)

- Headline

- Name of event

- Very brief explanation of event

- Date of event

- Time of event (beginning and ending)

- Where event will be held

- Compelling reason why event should be covered

57| Journalists are the Target Audience for News Press Releases

When you are writing a news release, for the primary purpose of generating news media coverage, it is important to keep in mind that your target audience is journalists, not the end-use consumers of your product or service. Journalists aren't interested in the features and benefits of your product or service. They are interested in hearing why your product or service is newsworthy. To write an effective news press release, you must first come up with an angle, or "hook" that will catch the attention of journalists and inspire them to want to write about it.

Look at your product or service through the eyes of a reporter. Journalists are tasked with providing their readers or viewers with timely, useful information that is free from bias. Is there a way to tie your product or service to current events in a positive manner? Has your organization recently received an award? Did someone in your company recently publish a book or major article? Is your product or service the first of its type? Is there something new or unique about the product or service you would like to promote?

58| Only Send Newsworthy News Releases to the Media

Because press releases can be a powerful tool for search engine optimization and for marketing directly to consumers, writing and publishing press releases online frequently is an excellent strategy. However, in our efforts to create backlinks, fresh content, and stay in front of consumers, many of the releases that get written aren't actually newsworthy. In the realm of direct-to-consumer marketing and SEO, that is absolutely fine. However, when interacting with members of the news media, newsworthiness matters.

To maintain good relationships with contacts in the news media, it is important to send news releases to them only when the information truly is newsworthy. Your online PR strategy might involve generating at least one news release every week. This is fine, as long as you don't make the mistake of sending every release you write to the media.

Some PR people make the mistake of thinking they should send everything to the press, and let reporters decide what to cover. However, if you habitually send news releases to reporters and editors that aren't newsworthy, they will stop paying attention to anything you send to them. Don't send every press release you write to the news media. You should only send news releases to your media contacts when they actually contain news.

59| Questions to Ask When Selecting a News Release Service

There are many different news release services, each of which offers different options for distributing press releases. Some distribution services are free, some charge a per-release distribution fee ranging from a few dollars to hundreds of dollars, and others are subscription-based services. Some services exist primarily for the purpose of posting press releases online for search engine optimization purposes and others are designed for the specific purpose of getting your news releases into the hands of the right reporters at the right time.

There is no single "best" news release service, because each type of service serves different purposes. Some companies utilize different services for different news releases. For example, a company responding to a crisis situation might use one of the more expensive services because of its extensive media reach and guaranteed fast delivery. The same company might publish general interest press releases that are not time sensitive via free news release services every week.

Questions to ask when deciding which news release service meets your needs:

- Is inclusion guaranteed within a certain period of time?

- How reputable is the service among the media?

- Can I target distribution geographically?

- Can I target distribution by industry?

- Does it reach trade or consumer audiences, or both?

- How much does it cost?

- Am I able to track results?

- Will the service write my news releases for me?

- Will my news release be checked for errors before it is sent

- Does the service assist with keyword optimization?

- Will my content be syndicated?

- Will my news releases be posted directly to major news search engines?

- Will the news release be sent to bloggers, associations, political leaders, and other influencers?

You aren't necessarily looking for all "yes" answers to these questions. The more comprehensive a news release service, the higher the distribution fee will be. Find out the answers to these questions, and then determine which ones really matter for your particular situation so you can make the best and most cost effective decision.

60| Top 4 News Release Submission Tips

- **Keep it Relevant** - Don't send the food editor of your paper a news release about a new motor oil unless it's edible. Send the new motor oil information to the reporter who covers automotive technology. If you waste a reporter's time with irrelevant information, he or she will just start ignoring everything you send.

- **Know the Audience** - Be aware of who the readers and viewers are for a particular publication before sending news releases. For example, if your company teaches entry-level computer classes you shouldn't send news releases to computer magazines whose readers are highly skilled programmers and network engineers.

- **Think in Angles -** The same story may interest many different types of journalists, depending on the angle you use in the news release. You don't have to send identical news releases to everyone. For example, if you are promoting the grand opening of a new flower shop, the business editor may be interested in the new business angle, the wedding editor may be interested in a unique wedding service the shop offers, the real estate editor may be interested in the architecture of the building in which the shop is located, etc.

- **Make Sure Releases are Legible** - It is never acceptable to send a hand-written news release. Make sure that any faxed, mailed, or emailed news releases are legible. Make sure the font is large enough to read, will transmit clearly, and is professional in appearance. Script and cursive fonts are not professional. Designs, patterns, and animations are also not acceptable.

61| Top 4 News Release Writing Tips

News Release How-To: Top 4 Tips for News Release Writing

- **Inverted Pyramid Writing Style** - Start with the most important information, and work your way down to the least important details.

- **No Exaggerated Claims** - Stick with the facts. You may think that your company is the *best, most innovative,* or *truly amazing* organization in the world, but these terms do not belong in news releases. Remember: in the world of journalism, if it isn't verifiable, it isn't true.

- **Keep it Interesting** - Reporters receive tons of news releases every day. If yours doesn't capture and hold their attention, your story won't end up in print or on video. The headline has to reach out and grab the reporters attention, and the content has to keep them interested.

- **Tell the Whole Truth** - News releases should never contain false information and they should always be thorough. When writing news releases, make sure that the content covers the who, what, where, when, why, and how. Don't make reporters call you to request details that you should have included in the first place.

62| Build Your Own Blog for Powerful Online Public Relations

Blogs can be powerful public relations tools. When you create your own blog, you basically become a social media publisher with a powerful tool for communicating information to the worldwide online community. When you have your own blog, you control the content. Of course, you have to make sure the content is information that people actually want to read, or you won't have any readers.

There are many different ways to approach developing blog content for online public relations purposes. The least successful technique is to publish a steady stream of sales messages. That is a surefire way to keep people from reading your blog. Publishing useful tips, hints, suggestions, tutorials, articles, etc. that appeal to your prospective customers is a much better strategy for creating a successful blog. When the majority of the content is not sales-oriented, it is fine to publish the occasional online press release on your blog.

Blogs create online public relations opportunities in so many ways. When you launch your blog, you can distribute an online press release to promote it, which of course helps optimize it by creating backlinks to it. If you get a URL that is separate from your main website, you can help optimize your main site by including links in your blog post. Additionally, frequently updated blog content provides many opportunities for social bookmarking and keeps content fresh.

You can easily get free content from free article directories if you aren't inclined to write all of the posts yourself. Some of the posts should originate from your company, but it is perfectly acceptable to publish free articles. The best strategy for utilizing free content is to select interesting content written by non-competing individuals who share a target market with you. When you publish someone's work, email the author the link with a note thanking him or her for making the content available. This could lead to a mutually beneficial referral relationship over the long term.

63| Coordinate Online Public Relations with Offline Efforts

Your online public relations efforts should work hand in hand with your offline efforts. No matter where it takes place, public relations plays an important role in creating a company's image. The look and feel of your company's website and other online public relations efforts should be consistent with the look and feel of your offline marketing materials. They don't have to be clones of each other, but there should be striking similarities. After all, an important element of successful marketing and branding campaigns is message consistency.

For example, it should go without saying that you should only have one logo, and it should appear on all of your printed and online materials. If part of your corporate image involves the use of corporate colors, then those colors should be utilized on all of your marketing materials, from your website to your company's letterhead stationery, and everything in between. Don't send mixed messages by neglecting to make sure that there is consistency between your online public relations and marketing activities and those that occur in the offline arena.

64| Enhance Online Public Relations with an Online Newsroom

Many organizations who seek to take advantage of the full spectrum of online public relations benefits are creating online news rooms. The purpose of an online newsroom is to allow journalists easy access to relevant information about your organization any time they want it.

An online news room should contain media contact information, press releases, company background information, white papers, company executive bios and photographs, artwork available for reprint, speech transcripts, streaming video of news conferences and speeches, investor relations information (if applicable), and other relevant documents.

With an online news room, you reduce the possibility of missing out on being included in a major story because you were away from your desk when a reporter working under a deadline tried to call you at the last minute. If the information the reporter wants is published on your online newsroom, being unable to speak by phone won't be a problem.

An online news room can be part of your organization's main website, or it can be a separate website just for members of the news media. Even though the primary purpose of an online newsroom is to provide information to journalists, when creating one it is important to keep in mind that the general public will be able to access it easily if it is linked to your website, and may stumble across it if it a separate site. For this reason, it is a good idea to include a link to a FAQ page for consumer inquiries.

Having an online news room can save time for both PR people and reporters. It can also result in a significant cost savings in terms of the printing and postage expenses associated with dealing printed press kits in response to every media inquiry.

65| Forums as Online Public Relations Tools

Online forums that are frequented by members of your target audience are excellent resources for online public relations. No matter what industry you are in, it is likely that there are several well-trafficked forums that appeal to members of your target audience.

By registering for forums that reach people that are interested in what you have to offer, you have any opportunity to get to know prospective customers and position yourself as an expert in your field by posting comments, responses to questions, advice, etc. Many forums have introduction threads that encourage new members to introduce themselves to the community. Some even have sections dedicated to brief online press releases about members' businesses.

Additionally, most forums allow registered members to include links to their websites and/or blogs in their signature lines. People who like what they see can easily click through to your website to learn more about you and your business. As an added benefit, every time you make a post, you will create a backlink to your website.

It's important to remember that forums are online communities. Don't post only when you want something or have something to promote. The key to successful public relations through forums is to consistently participate in the discussion. When you first join, you should start out by offering advice and suggestions to established members in response to their questions. This will help establish you as a legitimate participant as well as help position you as an expert in your field. Participate consistently, and you'll begin to be accepted as part of the community.

When deciding which forums to join, look for ones that seem to have an active community. Check to see that there are several different threads with a good number of recent posts from multiple users. Make sure to read the rules for each forum you join, as they may vary among forums. Some may require users to make a certain number of posts before including links in their signature lines, and others don't allow links at all.

66| How to Optimize Online Press Releases

By making sure that your online press releases are properly optimized prior to distribution, you can benefit from increased exposure to reporters and consumers, as well as improvements in your website's search engine rankings. The most important elements in press release optimization are: (1) link building, (2) proper use of critical keywords, and (3) compelling content.

Link Building

If you send out press releases that don't include links to your website in the body of your news release, you are missing an important opportunity to drive targeted, quality traffic to your website and to improve search engine ranking.

Do not assume that including a link in the contact information section of your online news releases is sufficient. The contact information section is often not published; in fact it is generally not intended for publication. Instead, it is intended to provide journalists with a way to get in touch with the author of the release for additional information.

Don't go overboard with links, however. One link per 100 words is the absolute highest number of links most you should include. Don't include links to every directory and subdirectory on your website. It is generally best to include links only to your home page or to landing pages with short, search-engine friendly URLs that are relevant to the content of the news release.

Critical Keyword Usage

The best way to make sure that qualified prospects see your online press releases is to write them with keyword optimization in mind. Don't make assumptions about the ideal keyword phrases to include in your content.

Do your homework and verify what types of keyword phrases people are using when conducting Internet searches for content similar to yours. You can check behind the scenes of your website to see which terms people are using to get to your site. You can also use the Treillian (www.keyworddiscovery.com) or Overture (www.inventory.overture.com) keyword selection tools to come up with ideas for frequently searched keyword phrases.

Compelling Content

Even though your ultimate reason for distributing press releases might be to increase your bottom line, journalists and Internet users aren't going to be interested in reading sales pitches disguised as press release content. If no one publishes your press releases, they won't be of benefit, no matter how many links or keyword phrases are included.

The information included in your press releases must provide value for the user. Remember that most Internet users are searching for information. If a press release provides useful, well-written information, readers are likely to be compelled to follow up with a visit to your website, where you may then try to sell your products and services.

67| How to Select Online Press Release Distribution Services

The fastest way to distribute press releases is with a wire service that specializes in online press release distribution. There are many different press release distribution services, and it can be hard to decide which service is the best one for your needs.

Tips for Selecting an Online Press Release Service:

- If you need writing assistance, select a distribution service that can handle writing for you.

- Press release distribution services that check their clients' online news releases for spelling, typing, and formatting errors prior to distribution can be very beneficial.

- A service that provides assistance with search engine optimization for your press release can help maximize results and exposure.

- It is a good idea to work with an online press release distribution service that assists with social tagging and social bookmarking.

- Be sure that any fee-based press release distribution service you use offers a direct feed into news search engines, to maximize your potential exposure to reporters and online publishers.

- The best press release distribution services provide targeted, direct-to-journalist distribution.

- Select a press release distribution service that provides RSS syndication.

68| Online Press Release Distribution Can Keep Content Fresh

One of the most important principles of effective online public relations and Internet marketing is the importance of fresh content. To keep Internet-savvy consumers interested in what you have to offer, you must continuously give them what they want and need. The main reason that most people use the Internet is to get information. Online press release distribution makes it easy to continually distribute and publish fresh content about your business or organization.

Once published online, content quickly becomes stale. One of the most important components of an online public relations plan is a constant supply of new content. Online press release distribution plays an important role in keeping content fresh. Any time a new press release is distributed online, to the media, or even published on the organization's own website, the potential for attracting attention, traffic, and customers increases.

Writing and publishing press releases on your website frequently is an excellent way of keeping content fresh. This has important benefits in terms of attracting new visitors via search engines, because frequently updated content can improve search engine ranking. Fresh content can also help drive return visitors to your website. Internet users tend to frequently visit websites that are updated with fresh content on a regular basis. Repeat website visitors are very likely to quickly become loyal customers. However, if your website never changes, people are not likely to keep coming back.

Additionally, submitting your press releases to the media (as appropriate) and disseminating them via online press release distribution services keeps fresh content about your organization in front of consumers. Every time your press releases are published on another website, assuming that your site's URL is included, a backlink is created to your website. This gives interested customers a means of quickly getting to your site, and also helps further improve your site's search engine ranking.

69| Online Public Relations for Direct-to-Consumer Communication

The growth of the Internet as a communications tool has greatly impacted the practice of public relations. In the days before the Internet became the powerful information and entertainment medium that it is today, the driving force behind most public relations campaigns was media coverage. Media coverage is, of course, still very much a part of public relations. Many press releases are still written and distributed for the purpose of generating coverage in traditional media outlets, such as newspaper, television, and radio.

Online press release distribution has added a direct-to-consumer element to public relations. Whereas the media once determined whether or not information would be made available to consumers, every organization with its own website can publish its own online news releases and other information. Online public relations enables PR practitioners to quickly distribute information to the media and to consumers simultaneously. In addition to submitting news releases to traditional media outlets, organizations are able to publish press releases on their own websites and distribute them widely via online press releases services.

Consumers are not as dependent on traditional media outlets for information as they once were. The Internet allows them to seek out and access the information they want at the exact times they need it. Smart public relations practitioners utilize online public relations techniques to get their messages in front of the right consumers at the right times.

70| 10 Top Viral Marketing Techniques

Viral marketing isn't expensive, yet it can bring powerful results to your bottom line. Here are 10 simple viral marketing techniques that anyone with a website can implement.

- Write articles that include links to your website in an author's resource box. Distribute them through directories that ezine and website publishers frequent in search of free content.

- Implement an affiliate program that compensates other website owners for referring traffic, customers, and/or subscribers to your website.

- Send out a news release or email campaign promoting a free download, product, or service available via your website.

- Publish an informative ezine and encourage readers to forward it to their contacts.

- Trade advertisements with non-competitive ezine publishers who reach consumers in your target market.

- Participate in social bookmarking sites such as Technorati, Digg, Stumble Upon, etc.

- Make it easier for readers to submit your website content to social media websites by including social bookmarking buttons as appropriate

- Publish content on high traffic user-generated sites such as Associated Content and HubPages, being sure to include a link to your website in your profile.

- Write eBooks and allow websites to give them away as subscription incentives.

71| Benefits of Viral Marketing

The purpose of online viral marketing is to create the online equivalent of word-of-mouth referrals for your business. A primary reason for utilizing viral marketing techniques is to benefit from the exposure that results from having people who do business with you, or come in contact with you, spread the word to their contacts about your business in the online arena.

There are many benefits to online viral marketing. It can create an online buzz about your company, and it helps your marketing messages reach people that you might not ever come in contact with otherwise. Viral marketing is inexpensive, and even free in many circumstances. There is also an important credibility component associated with viral marketing.

People don't always trust information they receive in email or come across online on their own, but if someone they know and respect shares information about an online resource with them, they are much more likely to trust its value and legitimacy. People tend to try things that their friends recommend. People tend to share positive experiences with their friends online and off, although it occurs with even greater frequency online.

72| Free Articles as a Viral Marketing Tools

Article marketing is a powerful internet marketing solution. This viral marketing technique involves writing articles related to your business and making them available to publishers for free reprint, provided contact information and a link to your website are included with the articles when they published.

Submit your articles to one (or more) of the many free article websites (such as www.ezineartilces.com or www.ideamarketers.com). Website owners, ezine publishers, and others frequently use these types of websites to find content that will appeal to their readers. Every time one of your articles is reprinted, your exposure to new prospective customers increases exponentially. Readers who are interested in what your article has to say are very likely to click through to your website.

The key to successful article marketing is to write interesting, keyword optimized articles that have information that people want. When publishers look for content to add to their websites, ezines, or other publications, they want content that is likely to drive people to their own websites or ezine subscription lists, and encourage viral marketing that benefits them. When your content is included, you benefit from their efforts to market their own business. It is a win-win situation for everyone involved. Publishers get free content that attracts visitors, site users get valuable information, and your organization is exposed to people who might never have found their way to you on their own.

73| Social Media Press Releases: Next Generation PR

Social media press releases are designed to meet the needs of journalists and consumers. Often referred to as the next generation of online publicity, social media press releases feature content (sometimes boiled down to bulleted text points), multimedia, links to additional content, social bookmarking tools, syndication subscriptions, and more.

With social media press releases, readers are able to bookmark and share information, sparking conversation and interest. Consumers benefit because they are able to actively participate in and track online communication about releases that interest them. Companies benefit from the viral marketing buzz that results from reader involvement. Journalists, bloggers, and other new media influences also benefit from social media press releases by having easy access to information, multimedia elements, and alternative research sources in a single place.

Boston PR firm Shift Communications is credited with developing the first social media press release template, which is available at www.shiftcomm.com. PRX builder (www.prxbuilder.com) is a tool for creating social media press releases. Users can easily create news releases in the WordPress based system, and distribute them via the PRX Releases (www.prxreleases.com) social media news release distribution wire.

74| The Secrets of Writing an Effective Press Release for Viral Marketing

Writing effective press releases for viral marketing campaigns is very different from writing press releases that are designed specifically to reach journalists or to be posted on news-oriented websites. Viral marketing press releases are direct-to-consumer communication tools by definition. When writing press releases for buzz viral marketing purposes, you have to really think about (a) what information consumers want and (b) what will inspire them to share the information with their peers.

- "Buy now and save" messages aren't appropriate for viral marketing. People aren't going to jump on the bandwagon of forwarding sales messages to their contacts.

- Provide valuable content that appeals to your target market. Remember that the focus has to be on value from the reader's perspective, not the company's.

- Don't mass distribute the same message to everyone. Instead, create individual messages for specific niche segments of your target market.

- Make sure your messages are well-written, error free, and appropriately formatted. You don't want to end up in a consumer-initiated "what not to do" viral marketing blitz.

- Provide some sort of incentive for consumers to pass along your content, such as a free whitepaper, eBook, software program, etc.

75| Tips for Successful Viral Marketing Campaigns

The primary objective of viral marketing campaigns is to spread a company's message and get people talking about it. Just like a computer virus can spread from one computer to another or a flu virus can spread from one person to another, viral marketing messages are intended to be passed along for exponential exposure. Viral marketing occurs any time people who receive information from or about your business pass it along to others. Viral content can include things like: ezines, newsletters, videos, advertisements, articles, pictures, testimonials, invitations to join online communities, and more.

Those who engage in viral marketing understand the power of information passed among peer, family, and co-worker groups. For creating buzz, viral marketing can be an unsurpassed internet marketing solution. However, not all attempts at viral marketing are successful. People who receive your marketing messages must pay attention to them, see value in them, and share them with others within their own spheres of influence for you to enjoy the benefits of viral marketing.

Internet Marketing Tips for Successful Viral Marketing

- Provide interesting content to people

- Provide content that people will want to share with others (tips, suggestions, humor, etc.)

- Provide a valuable service that people will want to share with their friends

- Give people incentives for sharing your messages with others

- Make it easy for people to forward content to others

- Make it easy for people to refer others to you

76| Tracking Viral Marketing Reach with Google Alerts

One of the most powerful tools for tracking the effectiveness of your online viral marketing campaign is the Google Alerts tool. This free tool allows you to receive email alerts when information about your company, or other topic of interest to you, shows up in relevant searches.

When you register keyword phrases from your viral marketing press releases, or other content, with Google Alerts, you will automatically be notified any time Google indexes new top 50 search results for those phrases. This is an excellent way to find out what people are saying about your company online as well as how frequently your organization is being mentioned.

For example, if you register "ABC Company" as a phrase with Google Alerts, you will receive an alert every time there is a new top 50 search result for the company. When you distribute press releases for ABC Company, you will be able to quickly determine where they are published and when, because you will receive an alert when each posting is indexed by Google. This tool also helps you track mentions in blogs, articles being picked up from free article directories, and more.

Google Alerts won't help you track offline publicity or press releases or ezines that are forwarded from one person to the next via email. However, it is an invaluable internet marketing solution for keeping up with online viral marketing. To get started, simply visit www.google.com/alerts and create alerts for up to 1,000 of the topics you want to keep up with online.

77| Viral Marketing with eBooks

Whether you give them away, sell them, or allow others to purchase master resell rights for them, eBooks can be powerful viral marketing tools. In order for eBooks to have benefit, from a viral marketing perspective, they have to (a) contain links back to your website and (b) contain useful information that people want.

Giving Away eBooks

Giving away eBooks can be an excellent incentive to get people to subscribe to your email list or to encourage current subscribers to refer their friends. There is so much SPAM and so many different email publications that people are often hesitant to give up their email addresses even when they are interested in receiving an ezine from your company. Offering a free eBook, that provides information they want, can be a great way to get them to go ahead and subscribe. Once they have subscribed, and they see benefits from your ezine and the eBook, they may refer contacts in exchange for additional or updated free eBooks.

Selling eBooks

Many people use free eBooks to provide just enough incentive to make readers want to purchase more detailed eBooks from their websites. eBooks that you sell should still include links back to your website. Purchasers who find them to be useful may refer others to your website, and may become repeat visitors in search of additional valuable information from your company.

Selling Master Resell Rights

Most people who own websites know the benefits of offering incentives for people to subscribe to their email lists, but don't have the time, skill, or inclination to write eBooks of their own. If you sell master resell rights of your eBooks to such individuals, you have created a win-win viral marketing strategy that can benefit you and the person who buys the rights to resell your eBook. Typically, once someone pays for master resell rights, he or she can brand the document, but the original links to your website remain intact. The purchaser can give it away as an incentive or sell it from his or her website. The end result is that the book gets into more people's hands, and can potentially refer countless first time visitors to your website.

78| Viral Marketing with Ezines and Newsletters

Well-written ezines and newsletters can be very effective public relations marketing tools. By creating and consistently distributing ezines and newsletters that contain valuable tips and interesting information, you can create a viral marketing buzz about your business that can drive more people to your website, increase the size of your opt-in subscriber list, and have a positive impact on your bottom line.

Viral marketing tips for ezines and newsletters:

- Provide quality content that people want (how-to tips, tutorials, free resources, etc.)

- Allow website visitors to preview content so they will know that they will receive valuable information for subscribing

- Offer an incentive to subscribe (such as a tip sheet or white paper)

- State that readers have permission to forward the document in its entirety

- Offer a bigger incentive to share with friends (such as an ebook, tutorial, free webcast, etc.)

- Reassure subscribers that you will not sell, rent, or give away their email addresses

- Include instructions for how to subscribe and unsubscribe

- Include a link or button for easy submission to social networking sites

- Make sure the document is professional in appearance and content (attractive, easy to read, free of errors, properly formatted, etc.)

- Distribute regularly, but not so frequently that people get annoyed (no more than once a week, at least once a month)

- Publish back issues of your ezine or newsletter on your own website

- Include your ezine or newsletter title in the company boilerplate section of your news releases

- Include your ezine or newsletter title in the author resource box for any articles that you submit to free article directories

79| Effective Business Communication Writing: Concise, Clear, and Direct

When writing a press release, keep in mind that you are not engaging in a creative writing process. Effective business communication writing is direct, to-the-point, clear, and concise. When writing press releases, and any other types of business documents, you must carefully consider the audience when structuring your messages. Stop and think about who your audience is before you begin writing, and choose terminology that readers are likely to understand without having to use a dictionary.

When writing a press release, you have to capture the reader's attention at the very beginning and tell your story as clearly and briefly as possible. Press releases should be written using the inverted pyramid writing style. Start with the most important information and work your way down to the least important information, which will conclude the document.

The most frequently overlooked rule of effective business communication writing is the necessary step of getting someone else to proofread your work before you send it out. When a journalist receives a press release that hasn't been properly checked for errors, the document is very likely to end up in the trash.

Also, many free press release services post documents online in the exact manner in which they are received. A press release riddled with typographical errors can become a permanent record of careless writing, which can have a negative impact on your organization's public image.

A great idea for a press release only becomes a great press release when it is written properly and distributed to the right people at the right time.

80| Financial News Releases are Important Tools for Investment Community

There are many different types of financial press releases. Simply visit the investor relations page of any publicly traded company and you will see a variety of financial news releases, including ones that document quarterly earnings, announce stockholders meetings or webcasts, analyst events, and more. Significant business changes for companies of all types are also documented through press releases. For example, merger press releases and acquisition press releases are issued to the news media and posted on company websites.

Stockbrokers, private investors, mutual fund managers, and others with vested interests in monitoring the financial progress of major corporations depend on a steady flow of financial news releases to get the information that they need in order to plan their investment strategies. Much of the information about significant business developments published in the Wall Street Journal, other financial publications, newspapers, industry magazines, and on the nightly news originated with a financial news release distributed through one of the major newswire services.

81| Kick Off Your New Company with a New Business Press Release

The first press release that any organization should send out is a new business press release. One of the best ways to spread the word about a new business is with the use of a well-written, widely distributed news release. As with all types of news releases, your new business press release should address the issues of who, what, where, when, why and how. It should state the name of the company, the primary line of business, where the business is located, when it will open, why it is an important addition to the economy, and how people can find it.

Regardless of the type of business you are opening, you should send your new business release to the business editor of your local daily newspaper. If you are a member of the Chamber of Commerce in your community, check to see if the organization publishes a newsletter. If so, your new business announcement will likely be considered for publication. If there are any other city, state, or county business publications, you will want to submit your press release to the appropriate editorial staff members.

You will also want to submit your news release to publications, other media outlets, and websites that reach your target consumers. It may be in your best interest to utilize a newswire service to make sure that you are covering all the bases in terms of getting your press release in front of the right people at the right time. You never get a second chance to make a first impression, and kicking off your new business with a widely published new business press release is a once in a lifetime opportunity.

82| Keep Your Eyes Open for Business Press Release Opportunities

The best way to generate publicity for your business is to keep your eyes open for any and every reason to write and distribute business press releases. Unless something bad happens, members of the news media aren't going to beat your door down to find out what newsworthy developments are occurring in your organization. Customers aren't going to call to ask you if you are doing anything new and different. If you are responsible for your company's public relations, it is your responsibility to let the public know what is going on with your business.

Remember that press releases serve many different purposes. In today's society, press releases don't have to be limited to documents that can be submitted to the news media. You don't have to send every press release you write to every contact that you have. Send ones that are genuinely newsworthy to your media contacts or distribute through a newswire. Others can be submitted to free press release websites, posted to your own website, and even included in your company's newsletters.

There are many reasons to write a business press release. For example, you can write business press releases announcing: new products or services, new clients (with their permission), new employees, launching a new website, employee of the month awards, anniversaries, consumer tips that tie in to your business, speaking engagements, employee accomplishments (such as publishing a book or article), and many other opportunities. If nothing interesting is going on, you can always plan an open house or work on a fundraiser with a charity tie-in. Good PR people are great at creating opportunities to generate publicity.

As the public relations voice for your company, keep your eyes open for information that you can share with the media and with consumers. Good PR people always look for the promotional angle associated with every day occurrences, and then come up with creative was to generate publicity.

83| New Hire Press Releases Are Great Publicity Tools

Adding a new key employee to your staff, or promoting an employee to a new position is a great way to generate publicity for your organization. It also lets your employees know that they are valued members of the team. Remember that an important component of any effective public relations plan includes elements of employee relations, and most people love to see their names in print.

When you add a new employee, simply write a new hire press release and send it to the appropriate media outlets. Send a promotion news release whenever you promote someone from within. Many local and industry publications, such as newspapers, chamber of commerce publications, and trade magazines have special sections dedicated employee promotions and new hires. Many of the free news release newswires and posting services also accept new hire news releases.

Use a standard press release template to format your new hire releases. The content should be brief and to the point. It should mention the company, the new employees name and credentials, and the position for which he or she was hired. Additionally, it is a good idea to include the company's website address to (a) make it easy for interested parties to find the company's website and (b) to enhance search engine ranking by creating a backlink assuming the news release is posted online.

Sample New Hire Press Release Content:

XYZ Corporation has hired Sue Anyone is Director of Employee Development.

Anyone has 10 years of experience in training and development in the healthcare and higher education. She has a Bachelor's degree in Business Administration and a Master's degree in Organizational Psychology.

XYZ Corporation specializes in employee benefits administration, serving clients in SOME CITY, AZ. For more information see www.XYZcorporationwebaddress.com.

84| New Product Press Releases Generate Trade and Consumer Publicity

When you release a new product, one of the best ways to let people know about it is to issue a new product press release. When writing a new product news release, keep in mind that you aren't creating a sales-oriented brochure. The key to creating successful new product press releases is to stick to the facts.

Tell the who, what, where, when, why, and how of your new product. If you can answer the following questions, you can write a new product press release: Who is introducing the product? What is the product? Where is it being made and where will it be available? Why is the new product beneficial? How can people learn more about it?

Both consumer and trade media outlets are generally interested in new product press releases, and there are many online resources for posting new product press releases. If your new product is of an industrial nature, you'll want to add www.productnews.com to your press release distribution list.

85| Positive Relationships with Journalists is Necessary for PR Success

As a PR person, you have to remember that it is in your best interest to cultivate positive, mutually beneficial relationships with reporters. One of the most important business communication tips for public relations practitioners is to remember the importance of treating members of the media with respect at all times.

Publicity is an uncontrolled form of communication. There is never any guarantee of media coverage in response to a press release, story idea, or special event. Too many PR practitioners burn bridges with journalists by behaving as if they have a right to expect, or even demand, coverage for their organizations. A reporter is never under any obligation to use a press release or a story idea, and will not likely respond well to pressure, nagging, or whining from a PR person.

When interacting with a reporter, it is vital to always observe proper business communication etiquette. In working toward establishing good relationships with journalists, you should be helpful without coming across as pushy. You should always return phone calls from reporters. You must demonstrate that you are a trustworthy and ethical, and you must never lie to a reporter. A PR person who loses the trust of journalists is not going to succeed in the long run.

86| Press Releases are an Affordable Promotional Tool for Small Businesses

For a small business, press releases can be the most effective and efficient means of promoting the organization. For many small businesses, especially new businesses and those with small budgets, buying advertising space and time is cost prohibitive. However, in order to grow, small businesses have to let consumers know who they are and what they do. Using press releases can be a very affordable solution that is often more powerful and effective than advertising.

In order to experience maximum benefit through the use of small business press releases, it's important to identify the media outlets and online resources that best reach the organization's target consumers. Get contact names and start building a solid, current media list. Observe the media carefully to find out what types of stories seem to get the most air time, ink, or bandwidth. Take a look at your organization to see what you might have to be offer that will interest the reporters, producers, and viewers. This will help you to determine what types of news releases can help you get the attention and coverage you need.

Small business press releases are just as likely to be published online or picked up by the news media as large company press releases. Armed with a creative mind and a good online, print, and broadcast media list, a small business owner or public relations director can generate a significant amount of media coverage for his or her organization.

87| Fashion Press Releases for Trade and Consumer Media

A fashion press release is one that is about products, events, trends, or news related to the fashion industry. There are different types of fashion press releases. A **trade** fashion press release is one that is intended to reach decision makers in the fashion industry. A **consumer** fashion press release is targeted toward end use consumers within the organization's target audience.

Trade fashion press releases are typically intended to reach:

- Retail buyers and managers
- Merchandisers
- Stylists
- Celebrities
- Movie Costume Designers

Consumer fashion press releases are typically intended to reach:

- Target population for a particular designer
- Target market for a retail outlet
- General consumer population based on appropriate age and demographics

88| Generating Publicity for Artists with Press Releases

Museums, galleries, arts festivals, and individual artists themselves often generate publicity by writing and distributing artist press releases. When your goal is to promote an arts-oriented event or business, one of the best ways to keep fresh content in front of prospective customers is to publicize participating artists and new exhibits. As an individual artist, distributing online press releases about your work and exhibits is a powerful way to build a name for yourself and increase organic traffic to your website.

Where to Distribute Artist Press Releases

Most newspapers have one or more reporters assigned to covering the Arts beat. There are also a number of publications dedicated to covering the arts and artists for both trade and consumer audiences. There are also a few online press release websites and distribution services specific to arts news releases.

For example, World Art Press Releases (www.e-worldartmedia.com) is an online press release site that features news releases specifically about art and artists. Art News Channel (www.artnewschannel.net) is a fee based press release distribution service specifically for the arts, offering online publishing and distribution to arts-oriented media contacts, museum curators and directors, art critics, art organizations, and art associations.

89| How to Publicize Special Events

Press releases can be an invaluable tool for promoting special events. Whether your event is local, regional, national, or even international in scope, there are many opportunities to attract attention as a result of writing and distributing an event press release. Before writing or deciding how to distribute an event press release, you need to stop and think about who you really want to reach.

For example, if you are hosting an invitation-only event, you aren't likely to be able to generate widespread promotional pre-event publicity in the mass media or online. Many media outlets will not print press releases for events that are not open to the public. It only makes sense that the media are more interested in communicating advance information to the readers about events that they have an option of attending than ones that are closed to them. You might, however, be able to get publicity for the event itself, particularly if a high profile individual is in attendance. For events that are open to the public, there are many opportunities for online and offline publication.
Event press release publication opportunities include:

- Many daily and weekly newspapers publish general event calendars that include listings of upcoming local events.

- Editorial sections of daily newspapers often include calendars of content-specific upcoming events (example: arts section prints artist press releases about scheduled exhibitions and theatre press releases for upcoming shows, etc.)

- Many television and radio stations have community event calendars on their web pages to which event sponsors or promoters can post press releases.

- Depending on the type of event you are promoting, you may also be able to include it on the website for your local chamber of commerce, convention or visitors bureau, city event calendar, etc.

- Producers at local radio and television stations may share information with on-air personalities based on event press releases, which can result in valuable broadcast mentions.

- Magazines often publish press releases about events that might be of interest to their readers. (example: *Southern Living* publishes an event calendar that includes home, travel, and cooking events held within the publication's primary distribution areas.)

- Bloggers who write about topics related to the events you are promoting will often publish information about upcoming events from press releases.

- Organizations that publish printed or electronic newsletters often publish information about events promoted by or of interest to their members. For example, the Mobile Alabama Arts Council (www.mobilearts.org) publishes an online calendar that includes information about all types of arts-related events in the local area.

90| Movie Press Releases: Promoting Films and Creating Tie-in Opportunities

How to Promote Movies with Press Releases:

Movie press releases play an important role in promoting the initial release of movies and publicizing initial and special edition DVD releases. Most major media outlets have editors and reporters assigned to covering the entertainment beat, and all entertainment press releases should be addressed specifically to these individuals.

There are also many celebrity and movie-oriented websites and blogs that accept movie and film press releases for publication. Such sites can be very valuable public relations tools for generating buzz about movie and film events.

How to Use Movies to Promote Your Business with Press Releases:

Businesses that are closely related to the subject matter of popular movies can capitalize on buzz about these films to write and distribute their own press releases with entertainment tie-ins. For example, the Wailea Beach Villas in Hawaii issued a press release announcing a "Nanny Survival Kit" to coincide with the release of the movie The Nanny Diaries. This marketing technique can be a great way to get a company's name in front of a new group of consumers. This type of press release might also be of interest to travel writers.

91| Musicians Benefit from Press Release Distribution

Music press releases offer individual musicians and bands an affordable means of promoting themselves. Whether a band has a CD at the top of the charts, or is a local cover band that plays at clubs, weddings, and community events, well-written and properly distributed music press releases can be a very effective marketing tool. Musicians who want to enhance their name recognition, audience size, and CD sales should definitely consider developing a public relations plan that involves consistently sending press releases to entertainment editors, reporters, and producers in their markets.

Types of Music Press Releases:

Promoting Shows: Many daily newspapers and entertainment-oriented weekly and monthly publications publish entertainment calendars. Additionally, many television and radio stations and other local events websites publish this type of information on their websites at no charge. Distributing band press releases announcing upcoming gigs to the right types of publications and websites can have a positive impact on awareness and show attendance.

Recording Release: Any time a musician or band releases a new CD, whether it is self-published or underwritten by a major record label, entertainment reporters are likely to be interested. Small bands that release CDs should send press releases to entertainment editors of all media outlets in the areas where they perform and/or have a following. Larger groups may be responsible for their own press release distribution, or may have the luxury of having an agent or manager to handle the details for them.

Signings : Musicians who hold signings at local record stores, coffee houses, clubs, etc. can utilize press releases to generate publicity for their recordings and the signing event itself. Many of the same types of publications that publish information about upcoming shows will also be happy to publish brief press releases about signings.

92| Sports Public Relations Career Opportunities

There are many types of public relations jobs in the sports industry, and this is a popular and fast-growing segment of the public relations profession. Sports public relations jobs are often referred to as sports marketing jobs. Some sports PR jobs are geared more toward scheduling and managing events, and others focus on media relations. Being a sports agent even requires public relations skills.

At the collegiate level, those involved in sports public relations often have the title of College Sports Information Director. Other common titles include: Director of Athletic Media Relations, Director of Athletic Media Communication, and others. The College Sports Information Directors Association of America (www.cosida.com) is the professional organization dedicated to this profession.

Sports public relations professionals handle many different responsibilities, including scheduling and organizing press conferences, distributing sports press releases, building and maintaining relationships with sports writers and broadcasters (and other journalists), arranging athlete and coach interviews, providing media communication training to coaches and players, crisis communication, and many additional opportunities.

Those interested in pursuing a career in sports public relations should consider getting education and/or experience in journalism, marketing, and sports management. Sports Management Worldwide (www.sportsmanagementworldwide.com) offers an eight-week online course for individuals interested in preparing for this type of career.

93| Targeted Online Entertainment Press Release Distribution with Billboard Publicity Wire

Billboard Publicity Wire (www.billboard.com) is an online press release distribution service that specializes in distributing entertainment press releases. Powered by PRWeb, a leading online press release distribution service, Billboard Publicity Wire can be a powerful tool for both online marketing and mass distribution music press release and other types of entertainment press releases to journalists and consumers.

With Billboard Publicity Wire, entertainment industry publicists are able to take advantage of many features specific to the industry. For example, music videos can be embedded within press releases and full electronic media kits can be attached. Releases can also be published on www.billboard.biz, the official website of Billboard Magazine.

Additional features include: production and distribution of Podcasts, Technorati tagging, RSS feed publishing (royalty-free), submission to major search engine news functions, distribution to opt-in email subscribers, posting to online news sites, and direct distribution to entertainment and music journalists.

94| Where to Send Book Press Releases

Distributing press releases is an important offline and online marketing technique for many types of products and services. Well-written, widely distributed book press releases can have a major impact on how well a book will sell online and in bookstores. Book press releases can even influence whether or not books even make it to the shelves of any book store.

When publicizing the release of a new book, it is important to write and distribute a book press release to the appropriate trade and consumer media contacts. Online distribution can also have a major impact on the success of a new book. It is a good idea to include a copy of the book along with the launch press release, so that journalists and other opinion makers have an opportunity to conduct a first-hand review of the publication.

Comprehensive book press release distribution typically includes:

- Trade magazines that target book retailers and retail buyers

- Book reviewers for consumer and trade magazines that reach the target market

- Book reviewers for major daily newspapers (USA Today, New York Times, etc.)

95| Always Use the Proper Press Release Format

It is important to use the correct press release format every time you create a press release. Reporters see hundreds of press releases every day, and using the correct format makes it easier for them to scan for the important information. If a reporter finds your press release difficult to read, he or she will simply move on to the next document.

Every press release you write should include the following components, in the stated order:

- Headline
- Summary Paragraph
- Body
- Company Details
- Contact Information

The headline should be written in title case and should include 170 characters or fewer. Do not put a period at the end of the headline.

The summary paragraph is a very brief synopsis of the news release, and should be written in complete sentences.

The body of your news release is the content. It should begin with the most important information, and be divided into paragraphs with no more than a few sentences per paragraph. At the beginning of the body, include your organization's geographic location and date the release is being submitted.

The company details portion of your news release is a very brief overview about your organization.

The contact information section simply includes information about how journalists can contact you for more information. Include the contact person's name, phone number, email address, company name, and website URL.

96| Company Information Boilerplate Should Be Standardized and Objective

The company information portion of your press release template is often referred to as a boilerplate. It is a brief, standard overview of your company that can include information such as: the company's name, its primary products and/or services, and the markets that the organization serves. There is no need to change the boilerplate from one news release to the next unless something in the information provided becomes incorrect.

The company information portion of your news release template should not be a sales pitch for your company. The company information portion of your news release should be written objectively and from a third person perspective. Unless what you are saying is a proven, verifiable fact, do not include it in your company boilerplate. Journalists are likely to question the credibility of the entire press release if this section is written from a sales-oriented perspective.

97| Don't Leave the Reporter Wondering if There is More

When submitting a press release via fax, an email attachment, or in printed form, it is important to notate that the document has ended or if the document is being continued on another page. Otherwise, the reporter who receives the document can't be certain that he or she has received the entire message.

Based on the guidelines for proper press release format, if your document is more than one page, you should type "-more-" at the bottom of each page except for the very last one. This indicates to the reporter that there is more information on a following page.

You should also let reporters know when they have reached the end of your document, whether it is just one page or if it is longer. In keeping with the guidelines for proper press release format, you should indicate that a story is over by typing "###" or "-30-" at the end of the document.

98| Line Spacing Matters in Proper Press Release Format

Using the right line spacing is an important component of the correct format for a press release. Press release documents should be single spaced, with a blank line between each paragraph. You should also leave a blank line between each section of the news release. For example, there should be a blank line between the heading and the summary, between the summary and the body, etc.

Do not hit enter at the end of each line. Instead, use the word wrap feature in your word processing program so that line breaks occur naturally. This is particularly important when you are submitting press releases online or via email. Unnecessary "enters" in a document can make it difficult for a reporter to copy and paste text from your news release into other documents.

99| Make Sure Journalists Can Contact You For More Information

Don't overlook including a contact person's name and phone number in your press release template. When you send out a press release, you need to make it as easy as possible for reporters to get in touch with you to request more information or to clarify the information in the release.

If you don't include your complete contact information on your news release, it is very likely that your story won't even be considered for publication. If a busy journalist has to take the time to track down a way to contact you, he or she is very likely to move on to a different story or find another source who is more easily accessible.

It is sound public relations practice to have a designated media spokesperson. If a journalist does take the time to track down your company's phone number, there is a good chance that he or she won't end up speaking to the right person at the organization. This can result in a reporter receiving information from a company representative other than what should be shared with a media representative.

Additionally, if you submit a press release that does not include complete contact details, the credibility of the information, and of your organization, may be called into question. A reporter will look at a press release that doesn't have a contact person's name and phone number as an anonymous tip rather than as information from a credible source.

100| Press Release Format Sends a Message

When preparing to format a press release, keep in mind that you are creating an important document that will be distributed to members of the news media. When you are writing for the media, you have a responsibility to follow the guidelines for effective media writing. Journalists are very busy, and they often receive hundreds of news releases every day. If you want a reporter to pay attention to your news release and consider it for publication, you at least have to submit a document that is formatted properly.

Additionally, it is important to keep in mind that every document that your organization creates and distributes plays a role in creating its image. Writing and distribute press releases is generally part of an organization's overall public relations strategy. One of the primary purposes and benefits of public relations is to create a positive image for the organization. By using the correct format for a well-written press release, you will send a positive message about your organization. An improperly formatted document, however, can convey a less than favorable impression of your company.

101| Save Time and Improve Consistency with a Press Release Template

Keep in mind that writing for the media is journalistic writing, not creative writing. While the content of each news release you write will vary, the proper format will not change. To be sure that your press releases are formatted properly and consistently, use a sample press release format to create your own document template.

By creating your own press release template, you will not have to worry about how to properly set up a news release each time you write a new one. The company information, geographic location, and contact information are not likely to change very often. Your sample press release format should include this information so that you just have to change the headline, summary, date, and body for each new document.

When you create your own sample press release template, instead of starting with a blank page every time you write a press release, start from your sample document. You'll save time and energy, and reduce the possibility for human error, when you use a pre-formatted template.

Every news release you write should follow the same format. By using a template to create your press releases, you won't have to stop and think about the proper format every time you write one.

The following press release template illustrates how each press release you write should be formatted:

[City] [State] [Service through which release is being distributed, if applicable] [MM/DD/YYYY] -- This is the body of your press release. The first paragraph should be your "hook," meaning that it should immediately tell journalists what is newsworthy about the topics. You have to catch their attention right away, or they will move on to the next story.

More Titles in the LifeTips Book Series

101 Entrepreneur Tips
by Susan Payton

101 Screenwriting Tips
by Alexis Niki

Printed in the United States
217221BV00004B/1/P

9 781602 750371